Crowded House

together alone

Folio © 1994 International Music Publications Limited
Southend Road, Woodford Green, Essex IG8 8HN England.
Music Transcribed by Barnes Music Engraving Ltd., East Sussex TN22 4HA
Printed by Panda Press · Haverhill · Suffolk
Binding by ABS · Cambridge

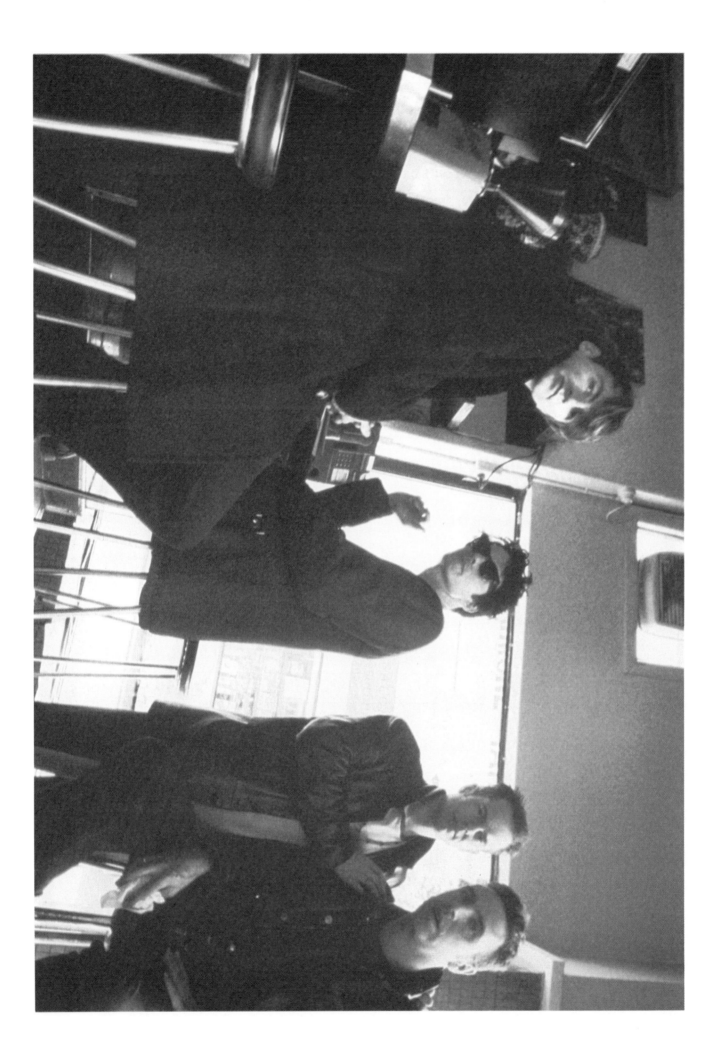

KARE KARE

I was standing on a wave
Then I made the drop
I was lying in a cave
In the solid rock
I was feeling pretty brave
Till the lights went off

Sleep by no means comes too soon
In a valley lit by the moon

We left a little dust
On his Persian rug
We gathered up our clothes
Got the washing done
In a long-forgotten place
Who'll be the first to run?

Sleep by no means comes too soon
In a valley lit by the moon

I was floating on a wave
Then I made the drop
I was climbing up the walls
Waiting for the band to stop
You can say the magic words
I got my sensors on
And this is the only place
That I always run from

Sleep by no means comes too soon
In a valley lit by the moon

KARE KARE

Words & Music by
Neil Finn, Mark Hart,
Nick Seymour and Paul Hester

I was feel-ing pret-ty brave till the lights__ went off.
In a long-for-got-ten place who'll be the first__ to run?

Sleep by no__ means comes too soon,__ in a val-ley lit by the moon,

yeah.__

9

_ means comes too soon,__ in a val-ley lit by the moon._____

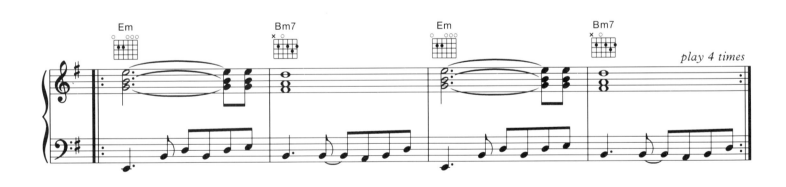

play 4 times

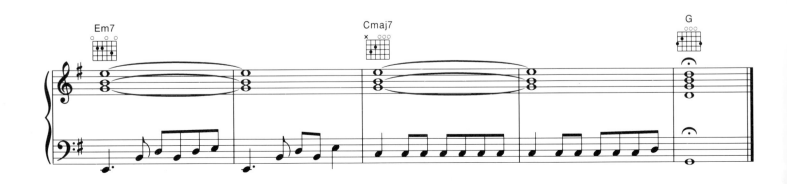

IN MY COMMAND

We're standing in a deep dark hole
Beneath the sky as black as coal
It's just a fear of losing control
You know so well
Don't miss it when the moment comes
Be submissive just this once
Imagine there is something to be done
Some truth to tell

I would love
To trouble you in your time of need
Lose your way
It's a pleasure when you're in my command

Juggle like a diplomat
Struggle to hold on to your hat
Swinging like an acrobat
But time will tell
The clock is dripping on the wall
Listen to the rise and fall
Close your eyes and hear the call
You know so well

I would love
To trouble you in your time of need
Lose your way
It's a pleasure when you're in my command
Put on your wings
You're responsible for everything

Desolate in anger or safe in isolation
You're about to be the victim of a holy visitation
By the rights I have been given

Put on your wings
You're not responsible for anything
I would love
To trouble you in your time of need
Lose your way
It's a pleasure when you're in my command

When you're in my command

IN MY COMMAND

Words & Music by
Neil Finn

14

NAILS IN MY FEET

My life is a house
You crawl through the window
Slip across the floor and into the reception room
You enter the place of endless persuasion
Like a knock on the door when there's ten or more things to do

Who was that calling?
You, my companion
Run to the water on a burning beach
It brings me relief

Pass through the walls
To find my intentions
Circle round in a strange hypnotic state
I look into space
There is no connection
A million points of light and a conversation I can't face

Cast me off one day
To lose my inhibitions
Sit like a lap-dog on a matron's knee
Wear the nails on your feet

I woke up the house
Stumbled in sideways
The lights went on and everybody screamed surprise
The savage review
It left me gasping
But it warms my heart to see that you can do it too

Total surrender
Your touch is so tender
You skin is like water on a burning beach
And it brings me relief

In the back row, under the stars
And the ceiling is my floor

NAILS IN MY FEET

Words & Music by
Neil Finn

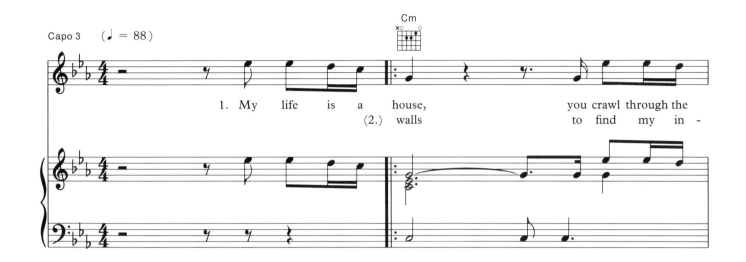

1. My life is a house, you crawl through the
(2.) walls to find my in -

win - dow, slip a - cross the floor, and in - to the re - cep - tion
-ten - tions, cir - cle round in a strange hyp - no - tic

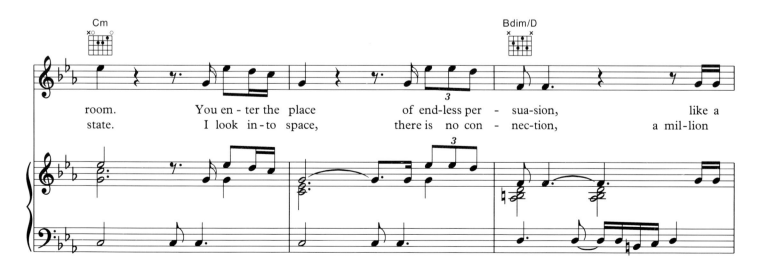

room. You en - ter the place of end-less per - sua-sion, like a
state. I look in -to space, there is no con - nec-tion, a mil-lion

knock on the door_ when there's ten or more things to do._ Who was that call -
points of light and a con-ver-sa-tion I can't face.   Cast me off one_

- ing?_____   You, my com - pan - ion_____
_ day_____   to lose my in-hi-bi - tions,_____

_ run to the wa - ter on a burn - ing_
_ sit like a lap - dog on a ma - tron's

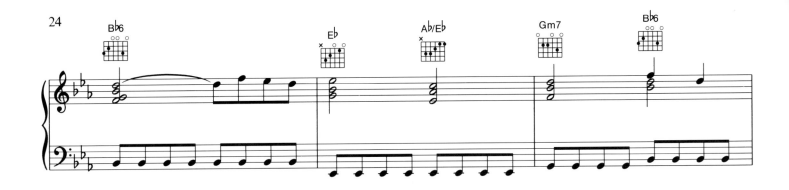

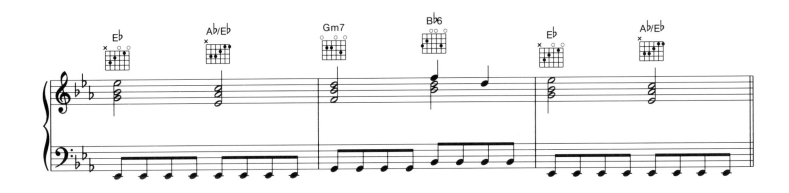

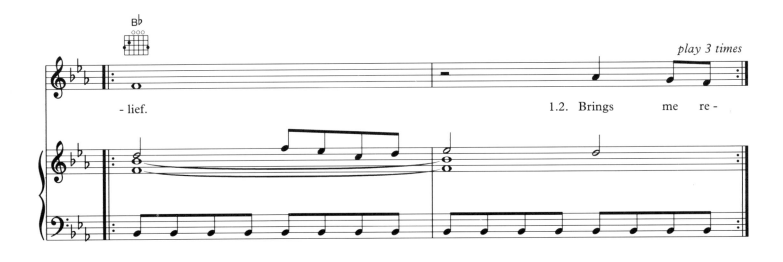

- lief.

play 3 times

1.2. Brings me re-

repeat ad lib. to fade

In the back row___ and un-der the stars,___ and the ceil-ing is my floor.

BLACK AND WHITE BOY

Black and white boy, black and white boy
You're so extreme, you're so confused
Colour me in, whatever mood I'm in
I could be still in touch with you

And you're full of the wonder of Spring
It's all sweetness and light that you bring
And a room full of people will fall to your infinite charm
But when darkness should quickly descend
You go quietly my miserable friend
To the depths of despair you will crawl

Black and white boy, black and white boy
You're so extreme, you're so confused
Colour me in, whatever mood I'm in
I could be still in touch with you

When you shake off the shadows of night
And your eyes are so clear and so bright
You make fools of the liars and creeps
Put a rose in my cheeks
But when demons have climbed on your back
You are vicious and quick to attack
And you put on a wonderful show
Do you really, really think I don't know?

Black and white boy, black and white boy
And you run like a cat to the cream
And you're acting so nice it's obscene
And you put on a wonderful show
Do you really, really think I don't know?
Black and white boy, black and white boy
Black and white boy, black and white boy

BLACK AND WHITE BOY

Words & Music by
Neil Finn

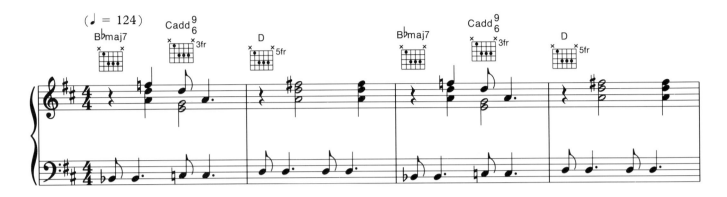

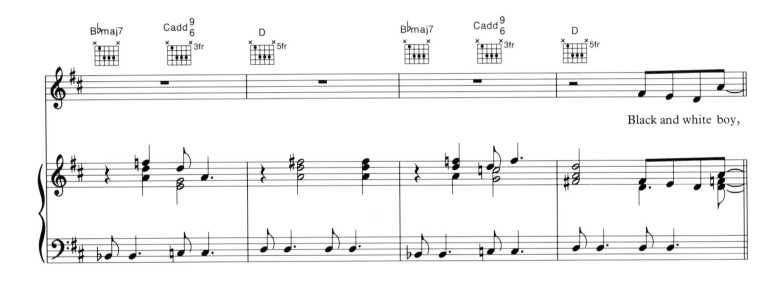

Black and white boy,

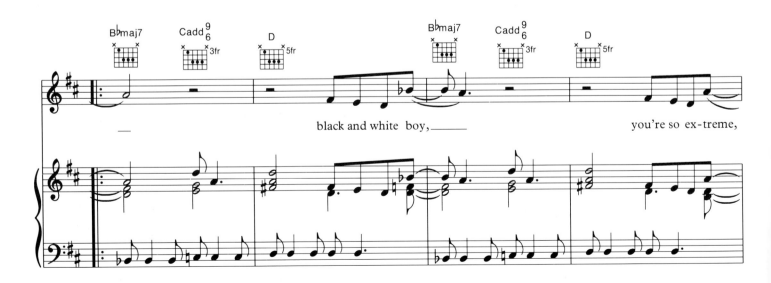

black and white boy, _____ you're so ex-treme,

ad lib. to fade

FINGERS OF LOVE

Can you imagine that
An itch too sensitive to scratch
The light that falls through the cracks
An insect too delicate to catch?
I hear the endless murmur
Every blade of grass that shivers in the breeze
And the sound, it comes to carry me
Across the land and sea

And I can't look up
Fingers of love move down
And I can't look back
Fingers of love move down

Colour is its own reward
Colour is its own reward
The chiming of a perfect chord
Let's go jumping overboard
Into waves of joy and clarity
Your hands come out to rescue me
And I'm playing in the shallow water
Laughing while the mad dog sleeps

And I can't look up
Fingers of love move down
And I won't be helped
Fingers of love move everywhere

And there is time yet
To fall by the way
From the cradle to the grave
From the palace to the gutter
Beneath the dying rays of the sun
Lie the fingers of love

Into waves of joy and clarity
A fallen angel walked on the sea
And I'm playing in the shallow water
Laughing while the mad dog sleeps

And I can't look up
Fingers of love move down
And I won't be helped
Fingers of love move everywhere

There is time yet
For you to find me
And all at once
Fingers of love move down

FINGERS OF LOVE

Words & Music by
Neil Finn

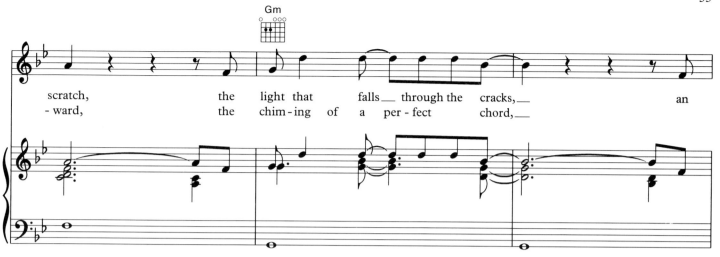

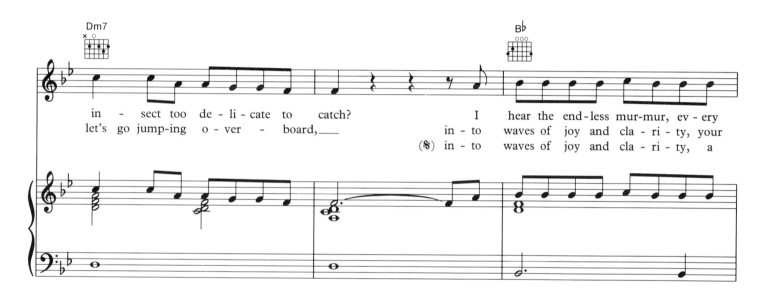

sound, it comes to car - ry me a - cross the land, and o - ver the sea,_____
play-ing in the shal-low wat - er, laugh-ing while the mad dog sleeps,_____
play-ing in the shal-low wa - ter, laugh-ing while the mad dog sleeps,_____

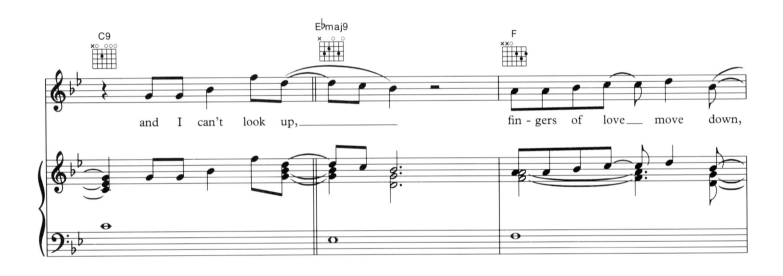

and I can't look up,_____ fin - gers of love__ move down,

_____ and I can't look back,_____
and I won't be helped,_____
and I won't be helped,_____

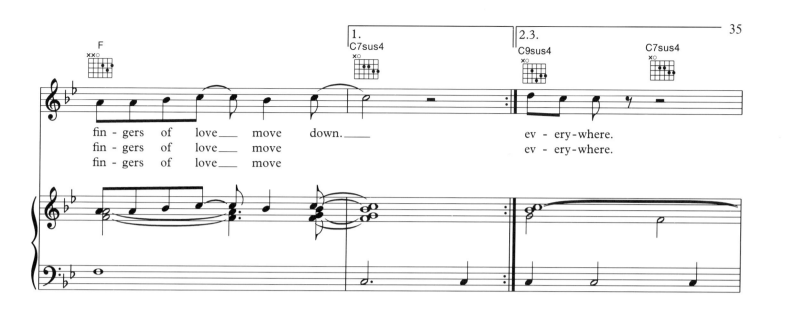

fin - gers of love___ move down.___ ev - ery-where.
fin - gers of love___ move ev - ery-where.
fin - gers of love___ move

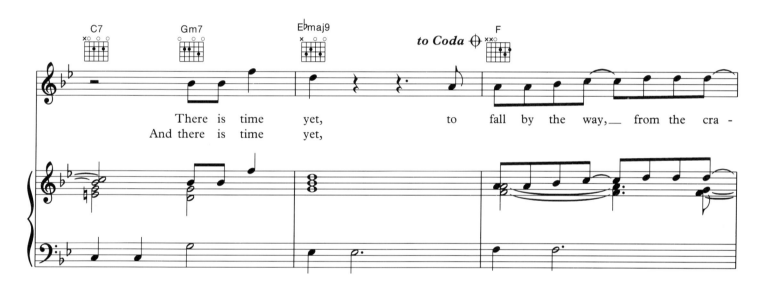

There is time yet, to fall by the way,___ from the cra -
And there is time yet,

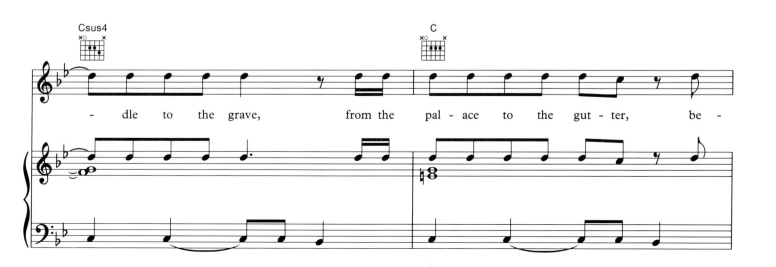

- dle to the grave, from the pal - ace to the gut - ter, be -

D.% al Coda

CODA

repeat ad lib. to fade

PINEAPPLE HEAD

Detective is flat, no longer is always flat out
Got the number of the getaway car
Didn't get very far

As lucid as hell and these images
Moving so fast like a fever
So close to the bone
I don't feel too well

And if you choose to take that path
I will play you like a shark
And I'll clutch at your heart
I'll come flying like a spark to inflame you

Sleeping alone for pleasure
The pineapple head, it spins and spins
Like a number I hold
Don't remember if she was my friend
It was a long time ago

And if you choose to take that path
I will play you like a shark
And I'll clutch at your heart
I'll come flying like a spark to inflame you

And if you choose to take that path
Would you come to make me pay?
I will play you like a shark
And I'll clutch at your heart
I'll come flying like a spark to inflame you

PINEAPPLE HEAD

Words & Music by
Neil Finn

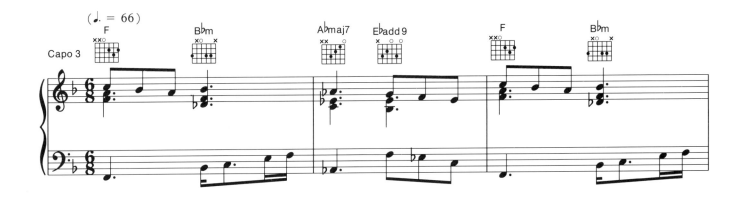

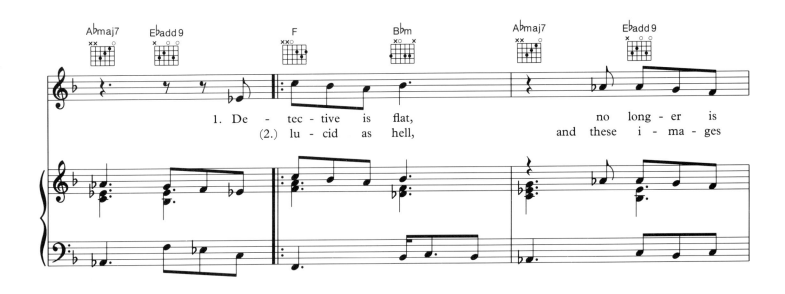

1. De - tec - tive is flat,　no long - er is
(2.) lu - cid as hell,　and these i - ma - ges

al - ways flat out,　got the num - ber of the get - a - way car,
mov - ing so fast,　like a fe - ver so close to the bone, I

42

LOCKED OUT

I've been locked out
I've been locked in
But I always seem to come back again
When you're in that room
What do you do?
I know that I will have you in the end

And the clouds they are crying on you
And the birds are offering up their tunes
In a shack as remote as a mansion
You escape into a place where nothing moves

I've been locked out
And I know we're through
But I can't begin to face up to the truth
I waited so long for the walls to crack
But I know that I will one day have you back

And the hills are as soft as a pillow
And they cast a shadow on my bed
And the view when I look through my window
Is an altarpiece I'm praying to for the living and the dead

Twin valley shines in the morning sun
I send a message out to my only one
And I've been locked out and I know we're through
But I can't begin to face up to the truth
I waited so long for the walls to crack
But I know that I will one day have you back

And I work with the bees and the honey
And every night I circle like the moon
And it's an act of simple devotion
But it can take forever when you've got something to prove

I've been locked out

LOCKED OUT

Words & Music by
Neil Finn

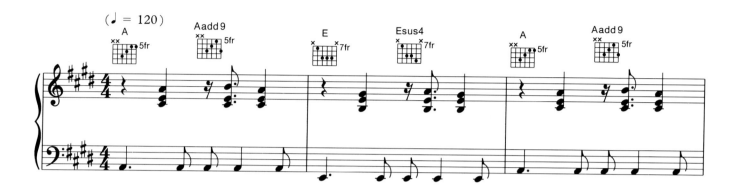

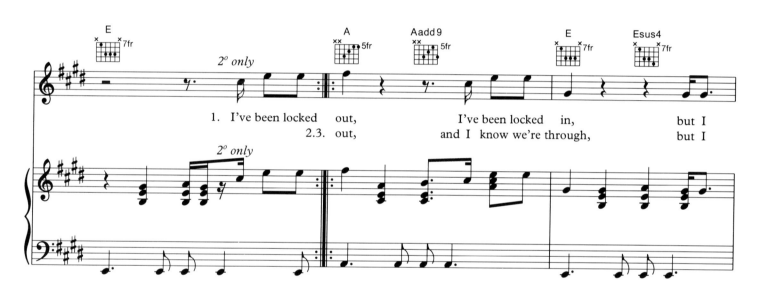

1. I've been locked   out,   I've been locked   in,   but I
2.3.   out,   and I know we're through,   but I

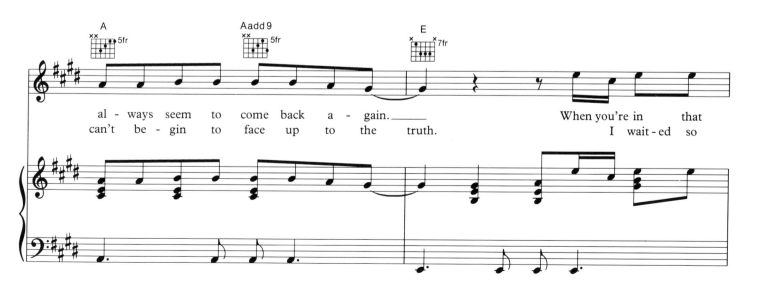

al - ways seem to come back a - gain._____   When you're in   that
can't be - gin to face up to the truth.   I wait - ed so

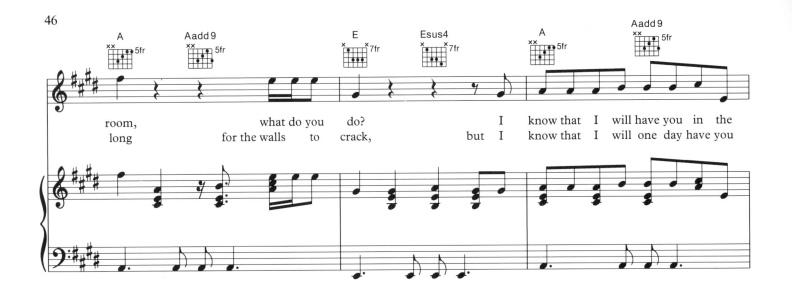

room, what do you do? I know that I will have you in the
long for the walls to crack, but I know that I will one day have you

end. And the clouds,____ they are cry-ing on you, and the
back. And the hills____ are as soft as a pil-low, and they
And I work with the bees and the hon-ey, and

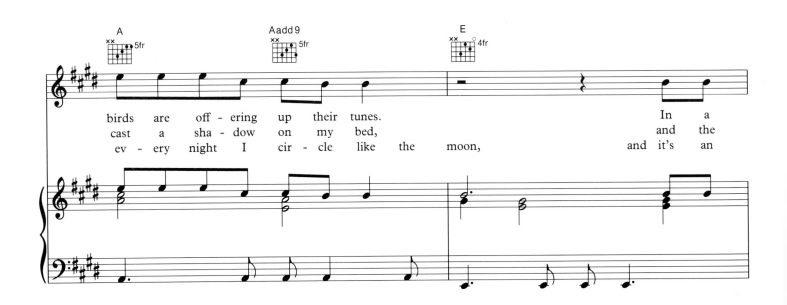

birds are off-ering up their tunes. In a
cast a sha-dow on my bed, and the
ev-ery night I cir-cle like the moon, and it's an

PRIVATE UNIVERSE

No time, no place to talk about the weather
The promise of love is hard to ignore
You said the chance wasn't getting any better
The labour of love is ours to endure

The highest branch on the apple tree
Was my favourite place to be
I could hear them breaking free
But they could not see me

I will run for shelter
Endless summer lift the curse
It feels like nothing matters
In our private universe

I have all I want, is that simple enough?
A whole lot more I'm thinking of
Every night about six o'clock
The birds come back to the palm and talk
They talk to me, birds talk to me
If I go down on my knees

I will run for shelter
Endless summer lift the curse
It feels like nothing matters
In our private universe
Feels like nothing matters
In our private universe

And it's a pleasure that I have known
And it's a treasure that I have gained
And it's a pleasure that I have known
It's a tight squeeze but I won't let go
Time is on the table and the dinner's cold

I will run for shelter
Endless summer lift the curse
It feels like nothing matters
In our private universe

PRIVATE UNIVERSE

Words & Music by
Neil Finn

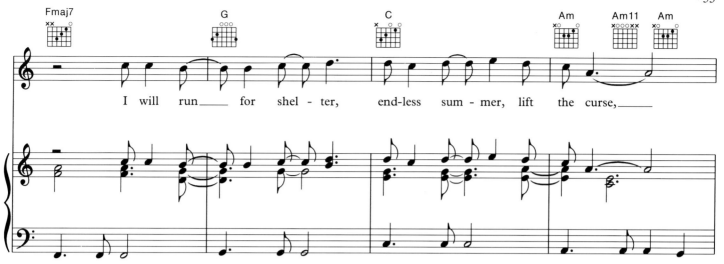

I will run_____ for shel - ter, end-less sum - mer, lift the curse,_____

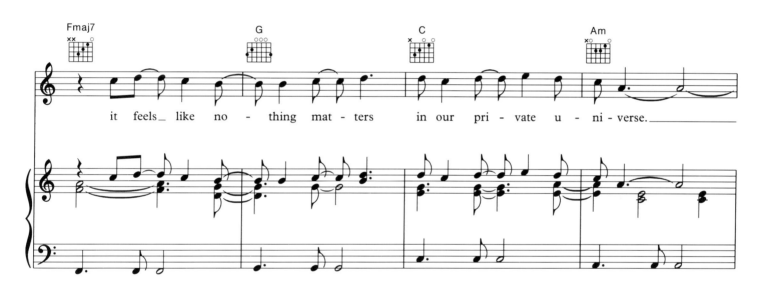

it feels_ like no - thing mat - ters in our pri - vate u - ni - verse._____

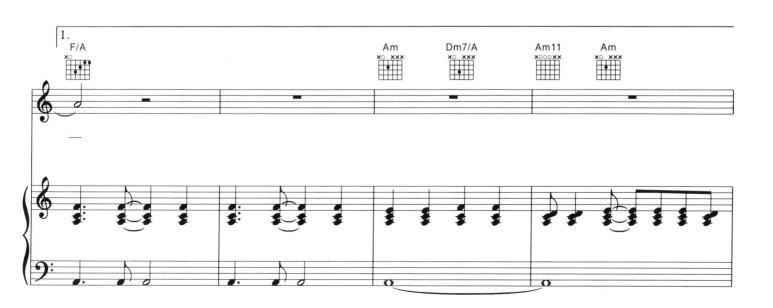

55

Time is on the ta - ble and the din-ner's cold.

And I will run___ for shel - ter, end-less sum - mer, lift the curse,___

it feels_ like no - thing mat - ters in our pri - vate u - ni - verse.___

- ni - verse.

repeat ad lib. to fade

WALKING ON THE SPOT

At odd times we slip
Slither down the dark hole
Fingers point from old windows
An eerie shadow falls
Walking on the spot
To show that I'm alive
Moving every bone in my body
From side to side

Will we be in our minds
When the dawn breaks?
Can we look the milkman in the eye?
The world is somehow different
You have all been changed
Before my very eyes

Walk around your home
And pour yourself a drink
Fire one more torpedo baby
Watch the kitchen sink
Lounging on the sofa maybe
See the living room die
Dishes are unwashed and broken
All you do is cry

Will we be in our minds
When the dawn breaks?
Can we look the milkman in the eye?
The world is somehow different
You have all been changed
Before my very eyes

Dishes are unwashed and broken
All you do is cry

WALKING ON THE SPOT

Words & Music by
Neil Finn

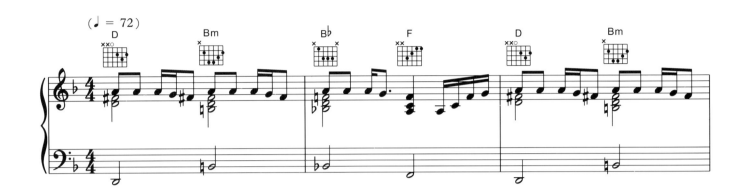

1. At odd times we slip, sli-ther down the dark hole,
2. Walk a-round your home, and pour your-self a drink,___

fin-gers point from old___ win-dows, an eer-ie sha-dow falls.
fire one more tor-pe-do ba - by, watch the kit-chen sink.

world is some-how dif-ferent, you have all __ been changed be - fore my ve-ry eyes. __

Dish-es are un-washed and bro-ken,

D.%. al Coda

⊕ CODA

rall.

all you do is cry. __

DISTANT SUN

Tell me all the things you would change
I don't pretend to know what you want
When you come around and spin my top
Time and again, time and again
No fire where I lit my spark
I am not afraid of the dark
Where your words devour my heart
And put me to shame, put me to shame

And your seven worlds collide
Whenever I am by your side
And dust from a distant sun
Will shower over everyone

You're still so young to travel so far
Old enough to know who you are
Wise enough to carry the scars
Without any blame, there's no one to blame
It's easy to forget what you learned
Waiting for the thrill to return
Feeling your desire burn
You're drawn to the flame

When your seven worlds collide
Whenever I am by your side
And dust from a distant sun
Will shower over everyone
Dust from a distant sun
Will shower over everyone

And I'm lying on the table
Washed out in the flood
Like a Christian fearing vengeance from above
I don't pretend to know what you want
But I offer love

Seven worlds collide
Whenever I am by your side
And dust from a distant sun
Will shower over everyone

As time slips by and on and on

DISTANT SUN

Words & Music by
Neil Finn

1. Tell me all the things you would change,
(2.) still so young to tra - vel so far,

I don't pre-tend to know what you want,
old e-nough to know who you are,

when you

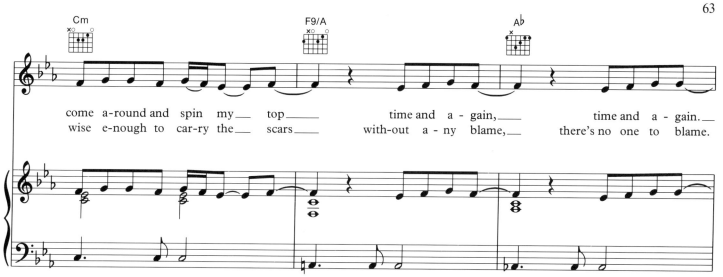

come a-round and spin my__ top_____   time and a - gain,___   time and a - gain.__
wise e-nough to car-ry the__ scars___   with-out a - ny blame,__   there's no one to blame.

_   No fire_____   where I   lit   my   spark, __
_   It's   ea - sy   to   for - get what you   learned, _

I   am not a - fraid of the dark, ___   where   your words   de - vour__ my heart,
wait-ing   for the thrill to   re - turn, ___   feel - ing your de - sire_____ burn, _

2. You're

sho-wer ov-er ev-ery-one,____ dust from a dis-tant sun__

will show-er ov-er ev-ery-one.__ And I'm

ly-ing on the ta-ble washed out, in the flood,____ like a Christ-ian fear-ing

ven-geance from a-bove,____ I don't pre-tend to know what you want,____ but I off-er love.

Se - ven worlds will col - lide_____ when -

CATHERINE WHEELS

No night to stay in
Bad moon is rising again
Dice rolls, you burn
Come down, I fear
As that cold wheel turns
I know what I know
Sad Claude's been sleeping around
To stroke the right nerve
Whose needs do I serve
As Catherine's wheel turns?

She was always the first to say gone
She's got her Catherine wheels on
Always the first to say gone
She's got her Catherine wheels on

Go kindly with him
To his blind apparition
Whose face creases up with age gone grey
You'll be back here one day

She was always the first to say gone
She's got her Catherine wheels on
Always the first to say gone
She's got her Catherine wheels on, wheels on

Catherine wheels
Catherine wheels
Catherine wheels

She's gone, vanished in the night
Broke off the logic of life
He woke, tore the covers back
Found he was empty inside
So they were told when the moon would rise
The best time to leave with your soul

She's gone up towards the light
Watching her whole life unfold
Bruises come up dark
So strong was his hold on her
Regarded by some as his slave
He spoke in a stranger's tongue
To spare us and drive you away
Bruises come up dark

CATHERINE WHEELS

Words & Music by
Neil Finn, Tim Finn
and Nick Seymour

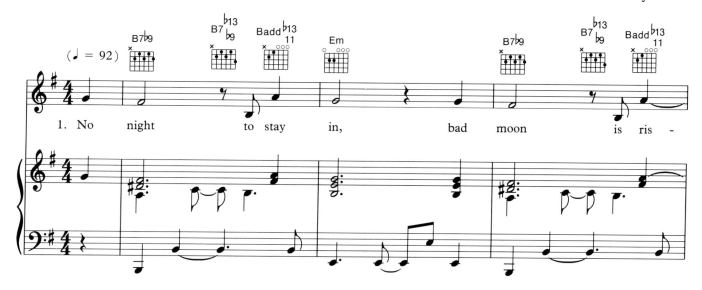

1. No night to stay in, bad moon is ris -

- ing a-gain. Dice rolls, you burn, come down.__ I fear__

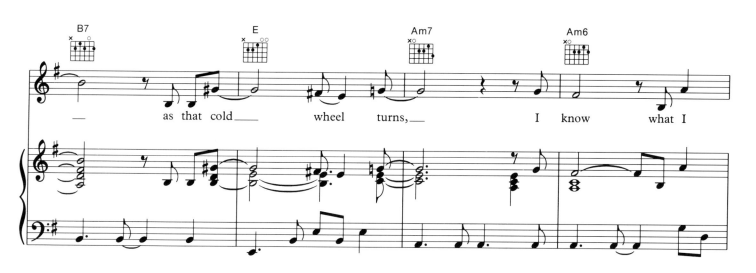

— as that cold__ wheel turns,__ I know what I

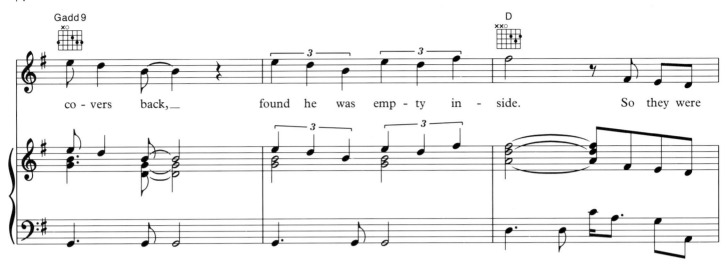

co-vers back,___ found he was emp-ty in - side. So they were

told when the moon would rise,___ the best time to leave with your
strong was his hold on her,___ re - gard -ed by some as his

soul. She's gone up to - wards the light, watch-ing her whole life un -
slave. He spoke as in a stran-ger's tongue, to spare us and drive you a -

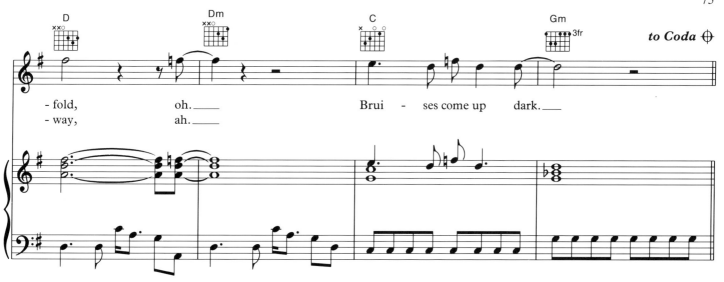

- fold,   oh._____   Brui - ses come up   dark.____
- way,   ah._____

to Coda ⊕

D.%. al Coda   ⊕ **CODA**

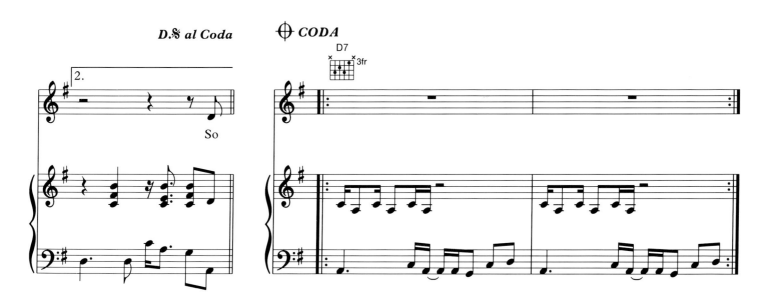

So

SKIN FEELING

I like the smell of that shop
I like the way it serves me
I like the pigment in your skin
I like the way it moves me
I like kids when they're asleep
Their little arms around you
I like the way you play games
Don't lose that skin feeling

I'm looking old, I'm feeling young
It's the truth my child
My second life has just begun
With this hungry girl

I like black and I like red
I like that orange circle
I like the things that you said
And when you were misbehaving
I like people on T.V.
But no one looks like me
I love you, you love me
Don't lose that skin feeling

I'm looking old, I'm feeling young
It's the truth my child
My second life has just begun
With this hungry girl

I love the pigment in your skin
I love the way it moves me
I like the smell of that shop
I like the way it serves me
I like the things that you said
When you were misbehaving
I love you and you love me
Don't lose that skin feeling

I'm looking old, I'm feeling young
It's the truth my child
My second life has just begun
With this hungry girl

It's the truth my child
Let me hold your hand

SKIN FEELING

Words & Music by
Paul Hester

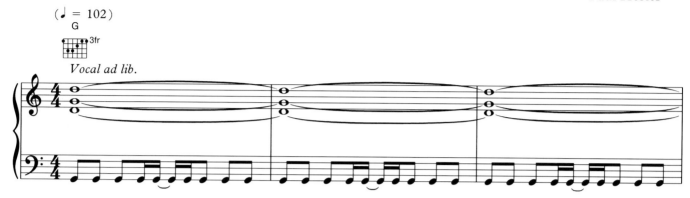

1. I like the___ smell of that shop,   I like the
2. I like black___ and_ I like red,   I like that
3. I love the pig - ment in your skin,   I love the

way it serves me.   I like the pig - ment in your skin,___   I like the
o - range cir - cle.   I like the things___ that you said,___   and when you were
way it moves me.   I like the smell of that shop,___   I like the

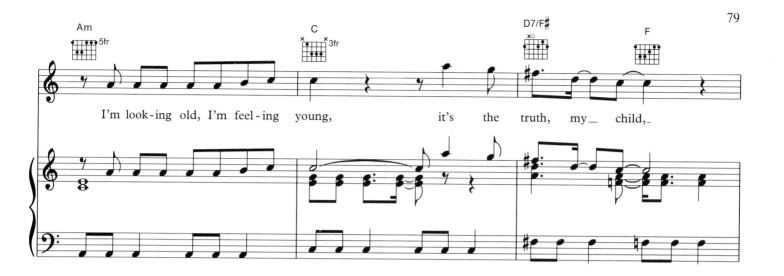

I'm look-ing old, I'm feel-ing young, it's the truth, my child,

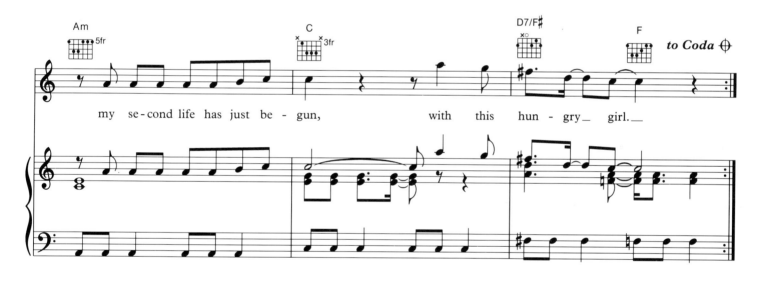

my se-cond life has just be-gun, with this hun-gry girl.

to Coda ⊕

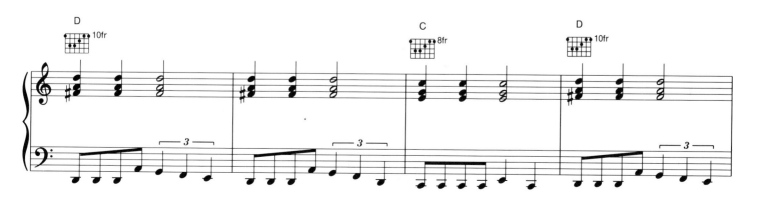

TOGETHER ALONE

Together alone
Above and beneath
We were as close
As anyone can be
Now you are gone
Far away from me
As is once
Will always be
Together alone

Anei ra maua
E piri tahi nei
E noha tahi nei
Ko maua anake
Kei runga a Rangi
Ko papa kei raro
E mau tonu nei
Kia mau tonu ra

Together alone
Shallow and deep
Holding our breath
Paying death no heed
I'm still your friend
When you are in need
As is once
Will always be
Earth and sky
Moon and sea

Maori Chant

Anei ra maua
E piri tahi nei
E noha tahi nei
Ko maua anake
Kei runga a Rangi
Ko papa kei raro
E mau tonu nei
Kia mau tonu ra

Translation:

Here we are together
In a very close embrace
Being together
Just us alone

Rangi the sky-father is above
The earth-mother is below
Our love for one another
Is everlasting

TOGETHER ALONE

Words & Music by
Neil Finn, Mark Hart
and B. Wehi

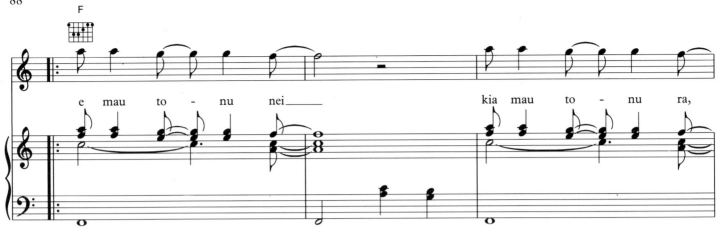

e mau to - nu nei_____ kia mau to - nu ra,

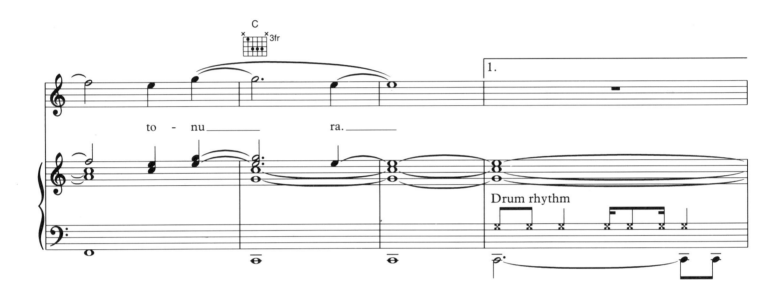

to - nu_____ ra._____

Drum rhythm

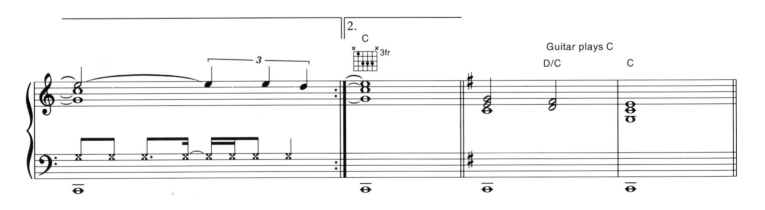

Guitar plays C

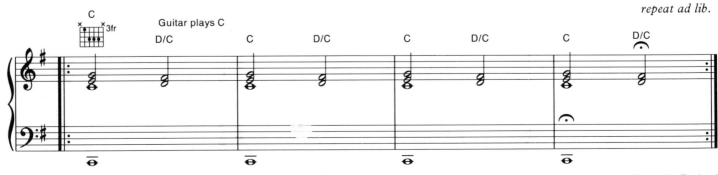

Guitar plays C

repeat ad lib.